Transcribed by TROY MILLARD

CONTENTS

	SONG	RECORDING
2	Artist's Foreword	
3	Transcriber's Foreword	
10	Avenue "D"	On The Corner
14	Backwoods	Sketchbook
18	Bertha's Bop	On The Corner
7	Change Of Season	John Patitucci
22	Growing	John Patitucci
26	On The Corner	On The Corner
32	Our Family	John Patitucci
40	Peace And Quiet Time	John Patitucci
37	Scophile	Sketchbook
42	Searching, Finding	John Patitucci
44	Spaceships	Sketchbook
48	They Heard It Twice	Sketchbook
50	'Trane	Sketchbook
56	Vaya Con Dios	On The Corner
60	Wind Sprint	John Patitucci

ISBN 978-0-7935-0763-4

7777 W. BLUEMOUND RD. P.O. BOX 13819 MILWAUKEE, WI 53213

Copyright © 1992 by HAL LEONARD PUBLISHING CORPORATION
International Copyright Secured   All Rights Reserved

For all works contained herein:
Unauthorized copying, arranging, adapting, recording or public performance is an infringement of copyright.
Infringers are liable under the law.

ARTIST'S FOREWORD

Hello!

First of all I'd like to thank you!! the reader/listener! Because of the kind letters I have received requesting printed music, and the research Hal Leonard Publishing has done, this book exists and is here to fulfill your requests. Now you'll also benefit from Hal Leonard's high quality printing, etc. and won't have to read my chicken-scratch.

I'd like to thank Dan Rodowicz and everyone at Hal Leonard for their enthusiasm about this project. Thanks for this great opportunity.

Many thanks go to Ron Moss for being a great manager/friend and for putting this project together in particular! Thanks to all at Chick Corea productions and Litha publishing. Thanks to Chick Corea, personally, for being inspirational as a musician and as my friend.

The Gold Medal for excellence in transcription, musicianship and patience goes to Troy Millard, an incredible bassist and dear friend who did an unbelievable job. Troy, I'm so very grateful and can't say enough about your talent! Thanks again. Thanks also to Lisa Millard, Troy's wife, for the great support and friendship. Thanks also to Larry Grenadier for a great job on the acoustic bass transcriptions.

Very special thanks to my wife Killeen, who is always encouraging and supportive of every musical project and who really understands this crazy music world.

To my family: Thanks to all of you for the years of support. Especially to my brother Thomas – my first teacher and inspiration to start playing bass.

Thanks to all of my teachers: Especially Chris Poehler, Charles Siani, Frank Sumares, David Baker, Barbara Johnson, Abe Luboff, Barry Lieberman.

Most importantly, this book is dedicated, along with every note I play or write to Jesus Christ, my Lord and Savior, who has given us all the gifts of life and music to share with each other.

Sincerely,

John Patitucci
11/8/91

TRANSCRIBER'S FOREWORD

John Patitucci's stunning virtuosity on both acoustic and six-string electric bass has garnered him the reputation of being the bass phenomenon of our time.

The solos included in the present volume constitute a virtual thesaurus of modern bass vocabulary. Careful study of these solos will greatly enhance the student's awareness of scale options, phrasing, thematic development and idiomatic expression. The student who wishes to acquire a virtuosic technique will also find the solos an invaluable aid in his or her development.

What follows is a brief analysis of John's style and some suggestions on how to study the transcriptions.

STYLE & ANALYSIS

SCALES

John's obvious command of scales and arpeggios in all keys and registers of the basses is the cornerstone of his prowess at negotiating beautifully melodic lines through all kinds of harmonic terrain. His ability to improvise harmonically complex melodies over relatively simple chord progressions or to reduce an impossibly dense chord sequence to a memorable and integral melody is the result of a highly developed sense of intuition based upon his broad knowledge of theoretical concepts and jazz history.

While it is not within the scope of this foreword to go into an in-depth discussion of these concepts[*], I would like to introduce the reader to some of John's "signature" melodies that incorporate exclusive use of some of the more commonly used scales in jazz today. All of the examples in this foreword refer to solos that appear in this book.

1. MAJOR

G♭ (F♯) Major (B Lydian)

("GROWING": Bar 52 of Solo)

A Major   E Major (A Lydian)

("GROWING": Bar 77 of Solo)

A♭ Major (D♭ Lydian)

("PEACE AND QUIET TIME": Bar 5 of Solo)

[*]A great source of information pertaining to this discussion is Mick Goodrick's "The Advancing Guitarist," also available from Hal Leonard Publishing Corp.

2. MELODIC MINOR

B♭ Melodic Minor

("WIND SPRINT": Bar 4 of Solo)

B♭ Melodic Minor

("WIND SPRINT": Bar 65 of Solo)

3. DIMINISHED

D Half Step/Whole Step

("PEACE AND QUIET TIME": Bar 14 of Solo)

(B♭ Passing Tone implies E♭ Melodic Minor)

The melody of "Scophile" is an outstanding example of creative use of diminished sounds.

PHRASING

John's sophisticated phrasing is a result of his study of the great jazz improvisers' approach to rhythm, particularly masters of the tenor saxophone whose fluid and legato style he strove to emulate. John cites saxophonists John Coltrane and Michael Brecker, and guitarist John Scofield as major influences on his development of his own unique voice.

To achieve this horn-like phrasing, John incorporates along with his formidable right-hand picking a left-hand technique that utilizes slurs, hammer-ons and pull-offs. This allows him to choose from a more varied rhythmic palette when "painting" a solo.

Some of John's favorite rhythmic devices are:

1. OCTAVE DISPLACEMENT* - **The use of open or ghosted C, G or D strings in conjunction with the upper registers.**

("SCOPHILE": Bar 92 of Solo)

("OUR FAMILY": Bar 20)

2. GRACE NOTES*

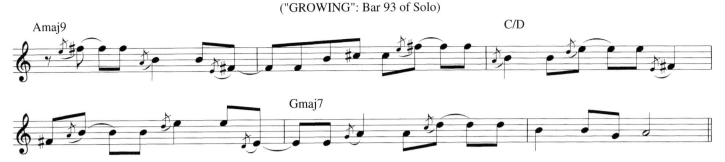

*These are also examples of subdividing the time. The emphasis or pulse becomes 3 instead of 4. (See No. 5 below.)

3. TWO AND FOUR NOTE GROUPINGS AS TRIPLETS

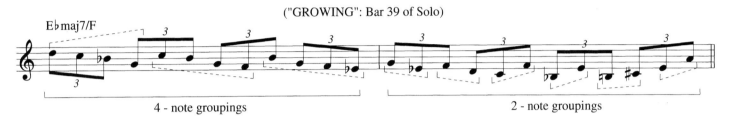

4. PLAYING OVER BAR LINE - Obscuring downbeat of next measure.

5. METRIC MODULATION - Emphasizing or grouping the notes of a line in a way that makes the time seem to change meter.

THEMATIC DEVELOPMENT

Thematic development refers to the process of creating a theme or motif and expanding on it, ideally to the point that its potential for evoking an aesthetic response in the listener is fully realized. John employs all of the common techniques used to achieve this end. Some of these include:

1. "Picking up" where the previous solo finishes (i.e. using the last theme stated as the jumping off point for his own solo). This is particularly useful if you view, as John does, the collective solos of all the performers as integrated parts of a larger, overall "solo" (i.e. the flow of the entire piece).
2. Repetition of the theme with slight rhythmic variation. This is especially effective when the theme is able to support many different harmonizations (i.e. the theme contains only notes that are melodically viable over many or all of the tonalities a piece presents).
3. Starting the solo with longer note values gradually changing to shorter note values or vice versa (rhythmic thematic development).

IDIOMATIC EXPRESSION

John's success as a working musician is due in large part to his comfort with and adeptness at interpreting different musical genres. From straight-ahead jazz to pop to Brazilian and other ethnic idioms, John is able to express himself fully while still maintaining the integrity of the idiom's roots. This is born out of a deep love and respect for different musical cultures and traditions. The result is a level of well-roundedness that anyone interested in making a career of music should aspire to. Even the most casual listening of John's work would reveal that he approaches each song keenly aware of its idomatic implications.

I would like to close the first segment of this foreword by reminding the reader that while this is a book of solos, the reader should by no means overlook John's marvelous bass lines on these songs. They make for an equally rewarding study and incorporate all of the aforementioned topics in their construction.

STUDY HINTS

Please notice that the majority of the transcriptions are notated in treble clef. This is due to the extended range of the six-string electric bass which spans four octaves. The written range of the six-string is B below bass clef to C above the treble clef. Like other basses, it sounds one octave lower than written. The logic of this notation becomes apparent in cases such as "Our Family" where both staves must be used to correctly notate the transcription.

In order to keep an already arduous reading task from becoming more so, articulations have been kept to a minimum. The recording itself should serve as the definitive guide in this department.

Traditional guidelines govern the use of accidentals except in those cases where enharmonic spelling of the notes might clarify John's choice of scale (i.e. if B♭ melodic minor is used over A7♯9(♯5), the ♯9 will be spelled C, the 3rd will be spelled D♭ and the ♯5 will be spelled F). The priority throughout is to make analysis of the line as it relates to the harmony as evident as possible. Frequent "reminder" accidentals are included in long passages to aid the reader.

Don't be dismayed by the speed at which some of the passages are executed. Great strides can be made if you practice difficult passages slowly and diligently to a metronome. Gradually increase the tempo as you become comfortable with the passage but strive for clarity and musicality at every tempo.

Low Gs and middle Cs that occur in a line that is otherwise an octave higher should serve as clues that these notes were probably played on open strings.

I would like to take this opportunity to thank John for being a great friend and teacher, Larry Grenadier for his superb transcription of the acoustic bass solos, and my wife Lisa for her support throughout this project. I hope you enjoy studying these solos as much as I have and I wish you the best in all musical pursuits.

Troy Millard

CHANGE OF SEASON

By JOHN PATITUCCI

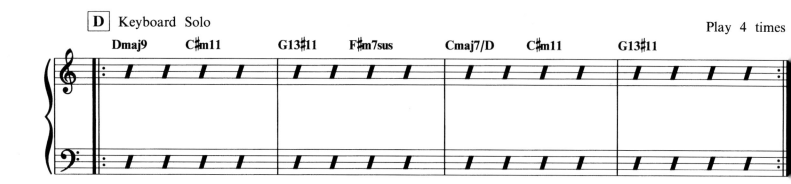

AVENUE "D"

By JOHN PATITUCCI

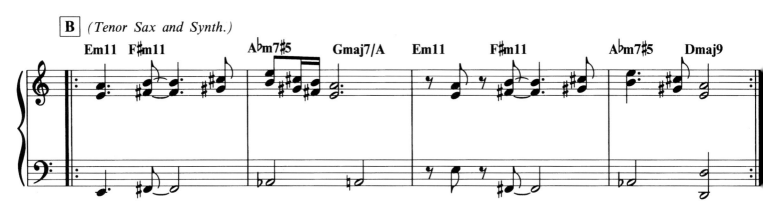

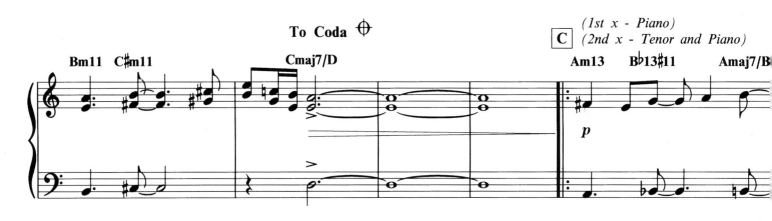

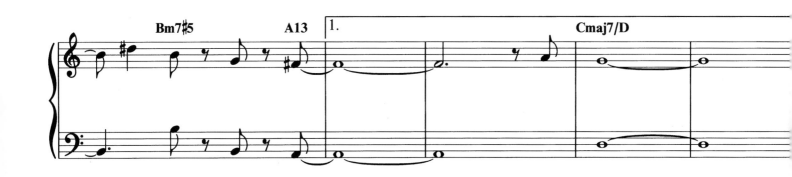

Copyright ©1989 LITHA MUSIC & ICCUTITAP MUSIC
International Copyright Secured   All Rights Reserved

BACKWOODS

SOLO ACOUSTIC BASS

By JOHN PATITUCCI

Moderately ♩ = 88

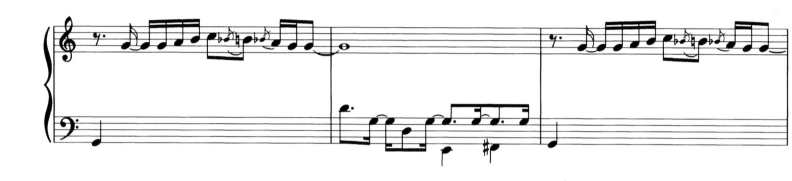

Copyright © 1990 LITHA MUSIC & ICCUTITAP MUSIC
All Rights Reserved International Copyright Secured

BERTHA'S BOP

Moderately fast swing ♩ = 212

By JOHN PATITUCC[I]

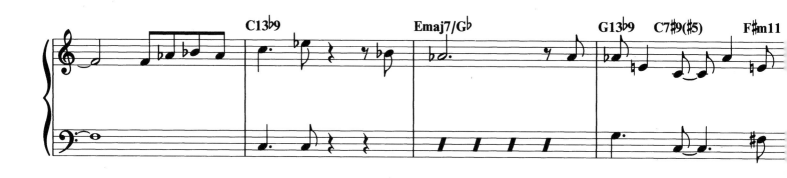

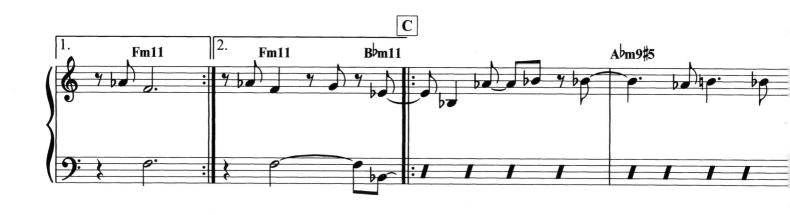

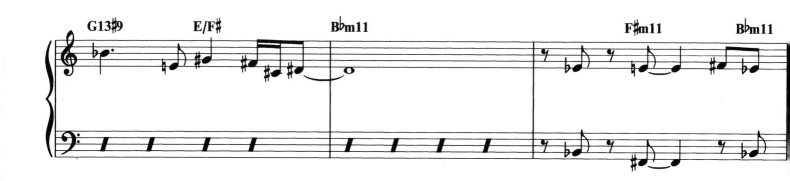

Copyright © 1989 LITHA MUSIC & ICCUTITAP MUSIC
International Copyright Secured   All Rights Reserved

ON THE CORNER

Funky Swing
♩ = 112

By JOHN PATITUCC

Copyright © 1989 LITHA MUSIC & ICCUTITAP MUSIC
International Copyright Secured   All Rights Reserved

OUR FAMILY

SOLO ELECTRIC BASS

By JOHN PATITUCCI

Moderately ♩ = 106

Copyright ©1988 LITHA MUSIC & ICCUTITAP MUSIC
International Copyright Secured   All Rights Reserved

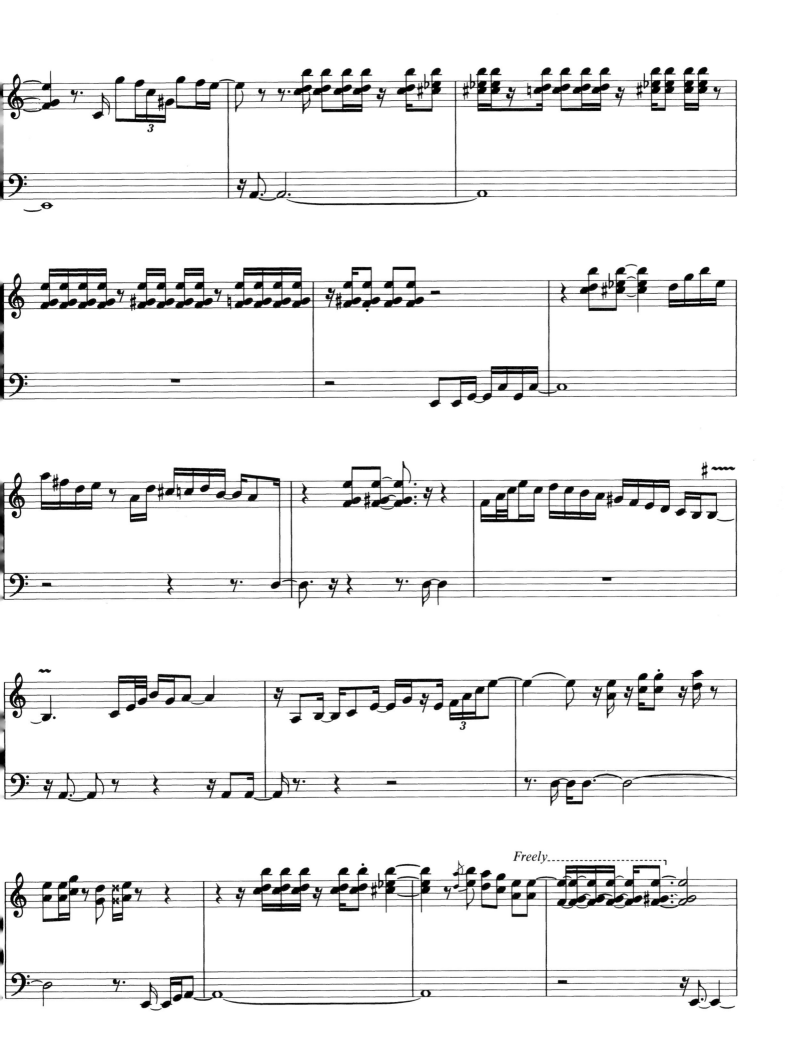

SCOPHILE

PEACE AND QUIET TIME

SEARCHING, FINDING

By JOHN PATITUCCI

SPACESHIPS

By JOHN PATITUCCI

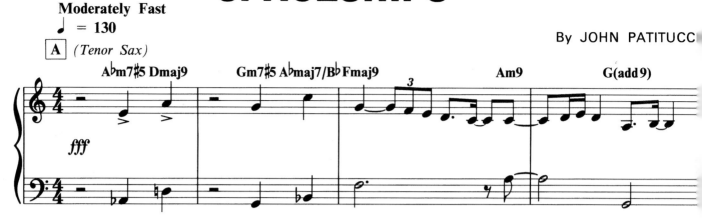

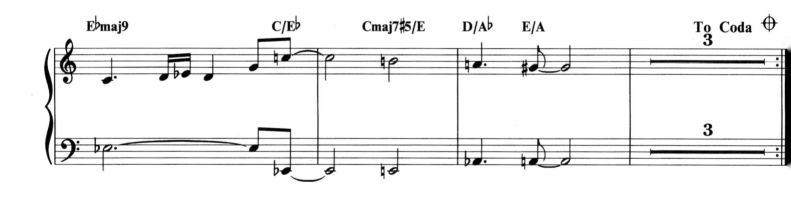

Copyright ©1990 LITHA MUSIC & ICCUTITAP MUSIC
International Copyright Secured   All Rights Reserved

THEY HEARD IT TWICE

By JOHN PATITUCCI

WIND SPRINT

By JOHN PATITUCCI

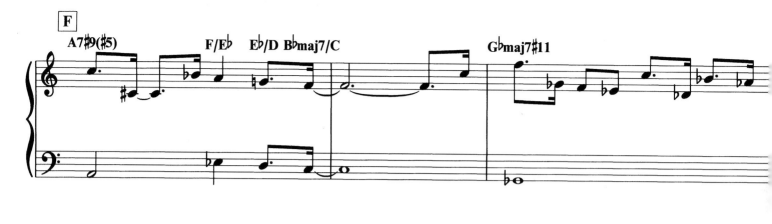

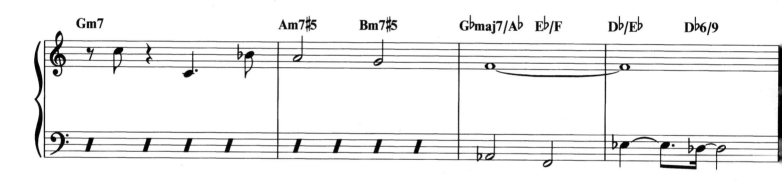
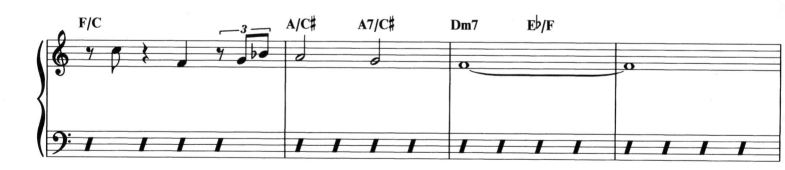
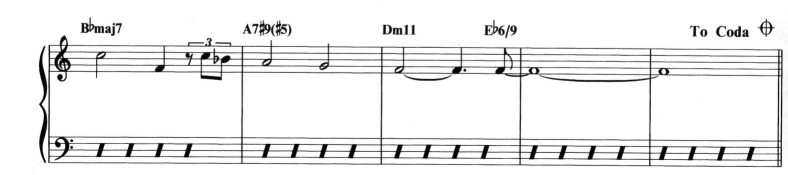